Beyond Mere Words

[handwritten inscription: To Jane Currie with a thousand good wishes Rev. Mac]

REVEREND MAC

This book is one of
a special first edition of 3000

Beyond Mere Words
My World of Flowers and Poetry

REVEREND WILLIAM McMILLAN

SPIRIT OF THE ROSE

Foreword

Julia Clements OBE,VMH
Life Vice President of NAFAS

Nothing gives me greater pleasure than to add a few words to this book as it portrays the work of our best-loved Reverend William McMillan.

Not only is his work inspiring but it is also technically correct and it has that extra something called *LOVE* which compels the onlooker to look INTO the flowers and not just AT them.

The Reverend Mac, as he is affectionately referred to, is very keen on the written word, and this, combined with his knowledge of flowers and plant material, make this a unique book, one very much after my own heart.

His thousands of followers in Britain and various parts of the world, especially the USA, where he is a popular lecturer/demonstrator, will welcome this book and I, as will they, wish it every success.

4

Julia

Beyond Mere Words
Reverend William McMillan MBE, MA, ML (GCA)

This book would not have been possible without the encouragement of my wife, Sheila and the drive and support of my son, Alastair. We were spurred on by the rest of the family, Jane, David and Andrew.

The professional skill of Annie Beagent and the photographic genius of David Lloyd have lifted my work into "… another world than this." I thank them most sincerely.

I am exceedingly grateful to Audrey Balderstone for her belief in this project. She and her husband David were not only lavish in their hospitality but consistently generous in their support and encouragement.

Special thanks go to Anne, Ian, Yolande and Father Sean. All in their separate ways were 'the wind beneath my wings' and I hope I have achieved what they believed I was capable of creating.

I am deeply indebted to my friends Eammon Kelly of Kelly Flowers International, (Northern Ireland), and Arie Durieux, Bloemenexport, Rijnsburg Flower Auction, Holland, who generously supplied all the plants and flowers. Patrick Kelly's interest was infectious and knew no limits. I am particularly grateful to him.

I also wish to thank Father P.J. Gormley SMA, who permitted some photography at Dromantine. Unfortunately it was not possible to include all the photographs taken there. Jill Grayston too deserves thanks for her meticulous proof reading.

To many throughout the world whose "… friendship through flowers" has enriched my life and whose enthusiasm for my presentations of 'Flowers with Poetry' inspired this book, I say a sincere thank you.

The Lamentation of the Old Pensioner

Although I shelter from the rain
Under a broken tree,
My chair was nearest to the fire
In every company
That talked of love or politics,
Ere Time transfigured me.

Though lads are making pikes again
For some conspiracy,
And crazy rascals rage their fill
At human tyranny;
My contemplations are of Time
That has transfigured me.

There's not a woman turns her face
Upon a broken tree,
And yet the beauties that I loved
Are in my memory;
I spit into the face of Time
That has transfigured me

W.B. Yeats

Masquerade

Can you sing, can you dance, can you play?
Always, always, always, live for today.

Come to the ball.
Dance through the hall.
A glorious play for all.
A mask is needed for this play.
Hide thine face, so you can stay.

Watch them twirl and dance.
Behind your mask, watch them prance.
Their eyes, oh their eyes, tell a story.
Of better days, of timeless glory.

…

Rick Wolfe

The Garden

How fair the flowers unaware
That do not know what beauty is!
Fair, without knowing they are fair,
With poets and gazelles they share
Another world than this

They can but die, and not betray
As friends or love betray the heart.
They can but live their pretty day
And do no worse than simply play
Their brief sufficient part.

Vita Sackville-West

From Endymion

A thing of beauty is a joy forever;
Its loveliness increases; it will never
Pass into nothingness, but still will keep
A bower quiet for us, and a sleep
Full of sweet dreams, and health,
and quiet breathing.

John Keats

He wishes for the Cloths of Heaven

Had I the heavens' embroidered cloths,
Enwrought with golden and silver light,
The blue and the dim and the dark cloths
Of night and light and the half light,
I would spread the cloths under your feet;
But I, being poor, have only my dreams;
I have spread my dreams under your feet;
Tread softly because you tread on my dreams.

W.B. Yeats

Morte d'Arthur

The old order changeth
Yielding place to new
And God fulfils Himself
In many ways
Lest one good custom should corrupt the world.

Alfred, Lord Tennyson

The Garden

...

How well the skilful gardener drew
Of flowers and herbs this dial new,
Where, from above, the milder sun
Does through a fragrant zodiac run;
And as it works, th' industrious bee
Computes its time as well as we!
How could such sweet and wholesome hours
Be reckoned but with herbs and flowers?

...

Andrew Marvell

30

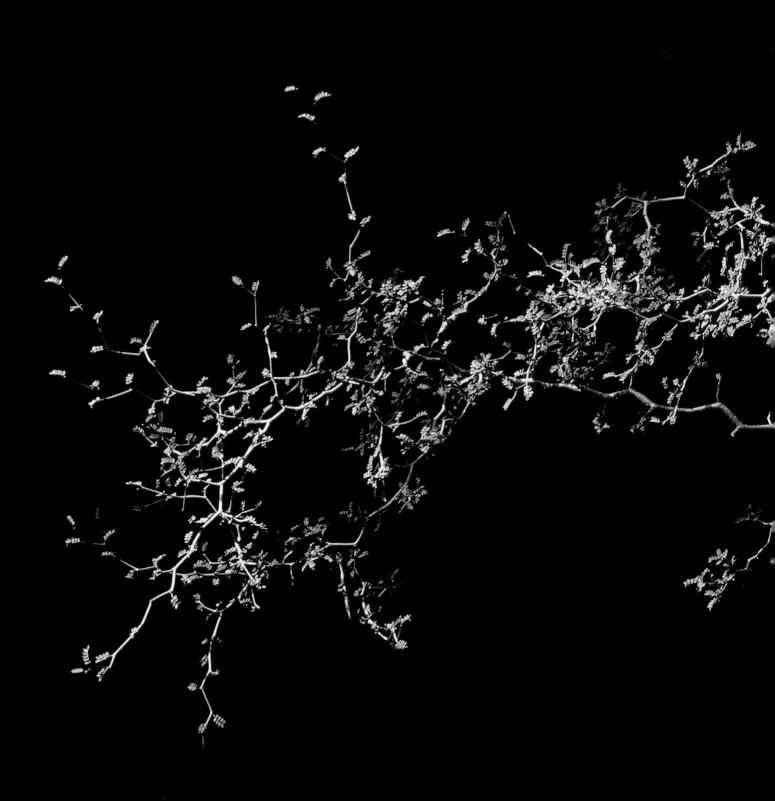

The Garden

…

Fair Quiet, have I found thee here,
And Innocence, thy sister dear?
Mistaken long, I sought you then
In busy companies of men.
Your sacred plants, if here below,
Only among the plants will grow;
Society is all but rude
To this delicious solitude

No white nor red was ever seen,
So amorous as this lovely green.

…

Andrew Marvell

The Mask

'Put off that mask of burning gold
With emerald eyes.'
'O no, my dear, you make so bold
To find if hearts be wild and wise,
And yet not cold.'

'I would but find what's there to find,
Love or deceit.'
'It was the mask engaged your mind,
And after set your heart to beat,
Not what's behind.'

'But lest you are my enemy,
I must enquire.'
'O no, my dear, let all that be;
What matter, so there is but fire
In you, in me?'

W.B. Yeats

42

Her Anxiety

Earth in beauty dressed
Awaits returning spring.
All true love must die,
Alter at the best
Into some lesser thing.
Prove that I lie.

W.B. Yeats

Sailing to Byzantium

An aged man is but a paltry thing,
A tattered coat upon a stick, unless
Soul clap its hands and sing, and louder sing
For every tatter in its mortal dress,
Nor is there singing school but studying
Monuments of its own magnificence;
And therefore I have sailed the seas and come
To the holy city of Byzantium.

W.B. Yeats

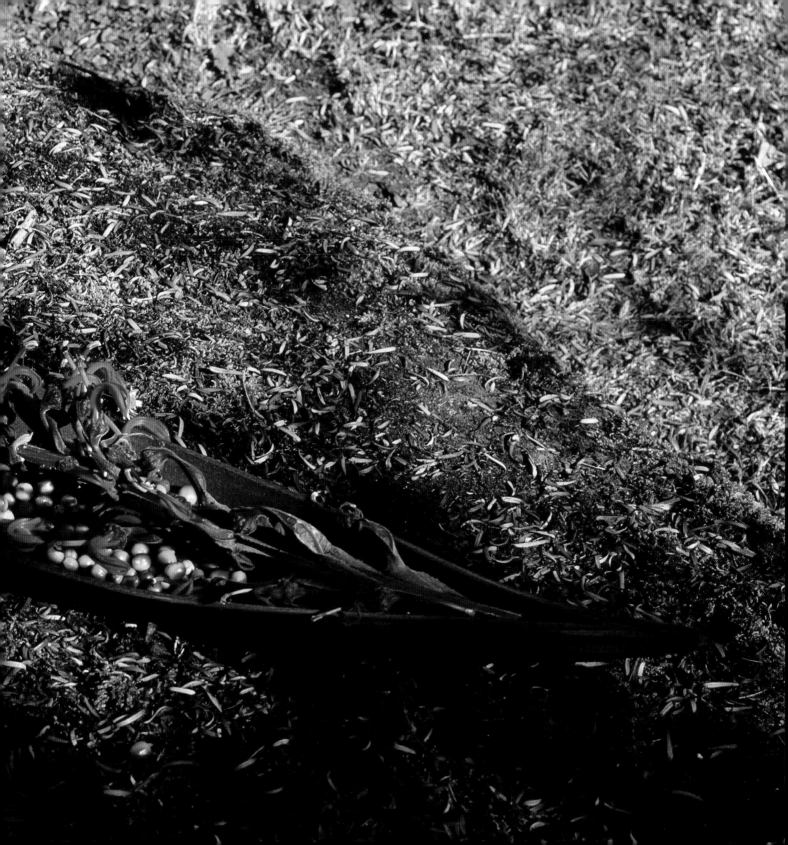

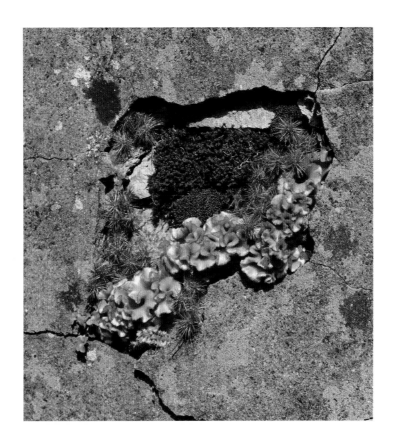

Flower in the Crannie Wall

Flower in the crannie wall
I pluck you out of the crannies
I hold you here root and all and all in all
In my hand little flower –
But if I could understand what you are
Little flower – root and all and all in all
I would know what God and man is

Alfred, Lord Tennyson

Imitations of Immortality

To me the meanest flower that grows
can give
Thoughts that do often lie too deep
for tears

William Wordsworth

For Anne Gregory

'Never shall a young man,
Thrown into despair
By those great honey-coloured
Ramparts at your ear,
Love you for yourself alone
And not your yellow hair.'

...

'But I can get a hair-dye
And set such colour there,
Brown, or black, or carrot,
That young men in despair
May love me for myself alone
And not my yellow hair.'

'I heard an old religious man
But yesternight declare
That he had found a text to prove
That only God, my dear,
Could love you for yourself alone
And not your yellow hair.'

W.B. Yeats

A Coat

I made my song a coat
Covered with embroideries
Out of old mythologies
From heel to throat;
But the fools caught it,
Wore it in the world's eyes
As though they'd wrought it.
Song, let them take it,
For there's more enterprise
In walking naked.

W.B. Yeats

Winter

Beauty's not always in a scarlet robe,
She wears an old black shawl;
She flouts the flesh and shows the bone
When winter trees are tall.
More beautiful than fact may be
The shadow on the wall.

Beauty's not always prinked in all her vaunt;
It pleases her to speak
In basic whisper to an ear
That will not find her bleak;
The hearing ear, the seeing eye
Who catch her signs oblique.

Vita Sackville-West

The Ballad of Reading Gaol

. . .

But neither milk-white rose or red
May bloom in prison-air;
The shard, the pebble, and the flint,
Are what they give us there;
For flowers have been known to heal
A common man's despair.

So never will wine-red rose or white,
Petal by petal, fall
On that stretch of mud and sand that lies
By the hideous prison-wall,
To tell the men who tramp the yard
That God's Son died for all.

. . .

continued:

For oak and elm have pleasant leaves
That in the spring-time shoot;
But grim to see is the gallows-tree,
With its adder-bitten root,
And, green or dry, a man must die
Before it bears its fruit!

. . .

It is sweet to dance to violins
Where Love and Life are fair;
To dance to flutes, to dance to lutes
Is delicate and rare;
But it is not sweet with nimble feet
To dance upon the air!

Oscar Wilde

Shipyard Philosophy

In this place of awful noises, where the creaking
gantries swing
Ugly arms across the spaces as their metal burdens
ring –
High above industry's clangour I have heard a lone
bird sing

And the hours of weary torture, toiling deep in
tank and hold,
Utter darkness all around you, ghostly fancies
manifold –
Then a beam of God's own sunlight brings a splash
of treasured gold.

Thomas Carnduff

The Fiddler of Dooney

When I play on my fiddle in Dooney,
Folk dance like a wave of the sea;
My cousin is priest in Kilvarnet,
My brother in Mocharvabuiee.

I passed my brother and cousin;
They read in their books of prayer;
I read in my book of songs
I bought at the Sligo fair.

When we come at the end of time
To Peter sitting in state,
He will smile on the three old spirits,
But call me first through the gate;

For the good are always the merry,
Save by an evil chance,
And the merry love the fiddle,
And the merry love to dance;

And when the folk there spy me,
They will all come up to me,
With 'Here is the fiddler of Dooney!'
And dance like a wave of the sea.

W.B. Yeats

The Harlots House

Like strange mechanical grotesques,
Making fantastic arabesques,
The shadows raced across the blind.

We watched the ghostly dancers spin
To sound of horn and violin,
Like black leaves wheeling in the wind.

Like wire-pulled automatons,
Slim silhouetted skeletons
Went sliding through the slow quadrille.

They took each other by the hand,
And danced a stately saraband;
Their laughter echoed thin and shrill.

Oscar Wilde

84

Red Hanrahan's Song about Ireland

The old brown thorn-trees break in two high over
Cummen Strand,
Under a bitter black wind that blows from the left
hand;
Our courage breaks like an old tree in a black wind
and dies,
But we have hidden in our hearts the flame out of
the eyes
Of Cathleen, the daughter of Houlihan.

W.B. Yeats

The Song of the Old Mother

I rise in the dawn, and I kneel and blow
Till the seed of the fire flicker and glow;
And then I must scrub and bake and sweep
Till stars are beginning to blink and peep;
And the young lie long and dream in their bed
Of the matching of ribbons for bosom and head,
And their day goes over in idleness,
And they sigh if the wind but lift a tress;
While I must work because I am old,
And the seed of the fire gets feeble and cold.

W.B. Yeats

Peace

Ah, that Time could touch a form
That could show what Homer's age
Bred to be a hero's wage,
'Were not all her life but storm,
Would not painters paint a form
Of such noble lines,' I said,
'Such a delicate high head,
All that sternness amid charm,
All that sweetness amid strength?'
Ah, but peace that comes at length,
Came when Time had touched her form.

W.B. Yeats

Plant Materials

Hydrangea macrophylla
Hypogymnia physodes

Lathyrus odoratus
Euonymus fortunei 'Silver Queen'
Jasminum officinale
'Argenteovariegatum'
Musa globba

Tropaeolum majus 'Empress
of India', Rosa 'Lambada'
Dendranthema 'Vyking'
Hypericum 'Envy Flair'
Acradenia frankliniae

Sophora japonica

Stipa gigantea
Hemerocallis 'Pardon Me'
Oncidium 'James Storey'

Kniphofia
Gloriosa rothschildiana 'Lutea'
Tropaeolum speciosum
Phormium Tenax Seedheads

Kniphofia
Gloriosa rothschildiana 'Lutea'
Tropaeolum speciosum
Phormium Tenax Seedheads

Hydrangea macrophylla
Celosia 'Bombay Yellow'

Dahlia. Alstromeria seedheads
Crocosmia seedheads
Viburnum opulus
Malus (Apples)
Solidago, Rubus fruticosus
Rhododendron bureaui

Rhododendron
Tropaeolum speciosum

Rosa 'Avalanche'

Rosa 'Avalanche'

Dendranthema
Rudbeckia
Pelargonium
Calendula
Cynara cardunculus

Zantedeschia 'Black Eyed Beauty'
Zantedeschia 'Purple Haze'
Zantedeschia 'Schwarzwalder'
Heuchera 'Palace Purple'
Fagus sylvatica - purpurescens group
Orchid 'Vanda'

93

Rosa glauca
Juniperus
Chamaecyparis
Trachelium 'Lake Superior'
Hydrangea macrophylla

Heliconia 'Black Prince'

Capsicum annuum
Heliconia

Guzmania 'Luna'
Palm seedhead
Seed pods

Orchid 'Vanda'
Malus
Forsythia

Orchid 'Vanda'
Reeds

Orchid 'Vanda'

Spohora japonica (Sophora...)
Taxus baccata 'Aurea'
Trachelium 'Lake Superior'

Dracaena
Aspidistra elatior 'Variegata'
Bupleurum fruticosum
Pisum - peas
Setaria

Aspidistra elatior
'Variegata'
Bupleurum fruticosum

Eryngium 'Supernova'
Steel grass

Strelitzia nicolai

Rudbeckia
Dried pods

Forsythia x intermedia
Rubus fruticosus

Phormium tenax seedheads
Phormium Hapene

Heliconia (dried)
Viburnum opulus
Succulents in variety

Coco Spathes
Heliconia veliger 'She-Kong'
Dried plant material

Coco pods
Anthurium 'Safari'

Vriesea
Phormium Hapene

Lobelia tupa
Hypericum androsaemum
Coco Spathe

Gloriosa superba 'Roth-schildiana'
Cornus alba

Hoya carnosa
Aeschynanthus 'Rasta'
Vriesea
Sansevieria 'Hahnii'
Sedum morganianum

Crassula in variety
Sedum in variety
Acaena microphylla

Celosia 'Bombay Pink'
Acaena microphylla
Moss

Rumex crispus
Phaseolus coccineus – scarlet runner beans
Nectaroscordum siculum subsp. bulgaricum

Gloriosa superba 'Lutea'
Sandersonia aurantiaca
Rosa 'Gold Strike'
Oncidium orchid

Sea grass
Rudbeckia

Zantedeschia

Lobelia tupa

Muehlenbeckia complexa
Celosia
Sedums

Dried leaf
Dried Fungi

Rosa 'Akito'

Tacca chantrierei (Black Bat Flower)

Juniperus
Tacca chantrierei
(Black Bat Flower)

Tillandsia xerographica

Muehlenbeckia complexa
Rumex crispus
Phormium Hapene
Gorgonian coral

Allium sativum var.
ophioscordon
Sedum

Corokia cotoneaster

Gloriosa superba 'Rothschildiana'
Miscanthus sacchariflorus
Punga Wood
Gorgonian Coral

Miscanthus sacchariflorus
Vitus vinifera - grapes
Tillandsia xerographica

First published in 2006 by
Spirit of the Rose Ltd
37 Woodlands
Witney
Oxfordshire
OX28 2DR

www.spiritoftherose.com

A catalogue record for this book is available from the British Library.
ISBN 0-9543939-1-0

96

Editor Annie Beagent
Text editor Jill Grayston
Project co-ordinator Audrey Balderstone
Scanning by Elizabeth Whiting Associates
Design and Production by Self Publish Solutions
Printed by Hill Shorter